ACHIEVING FINANCIAL FREEDOM IN YOUR 40'S

ACHIEVING FINANCIAL FREEDOM IN YOUR 40'S

Series "Financial Freedom at Any Age"
By: D.K. Hawkins
Version 1.1 ~November 2021
Published by D.K. Hawkins at KDP
Copyright ©2021 by D.K. Hawkins. All rights reserved.

No part of this publication may be reproduced, distributed or transmitted in any form or by any means including photocopying, recording or other electronic or mechanical methods or by any information storage or retrieval system without the prior written permission of the publishers, except in the case of very brief quotations embodied in critical reviews and certain other noncommercial uses permitted by copyright law.

All rights reserved, including the right of reproduction in whole or in part in any form.

All information in this book has been carefully researched and checked for factual accuracy. However, the author and publisher make no warranty, express or implied, that the information contained herein is appropriate for every individual, situation, or purpose and assume no responsibility for errors or omissions.

The reader assumes the risk and full responsibility for all actions. The author will not be held responsible for any loss or damage, whether consequential, incidental, special, or otherwise, that may result from the information presented in this book.

All images are free for use or purchased from stock photo sites or royalty-free for commercial use. I have relied on my own observations as well as many different sources for this book, and I have done my best to check facts and give credit where it is due. In the event that any material is used without proper permission, please contact me so that the oversight can be corrected

The information provided in this book is for informational purposes only and is not intended to be a source of advice or credit analysis with respect to the material presented. The information and/or documents contained in this book do not constitute legal or financial advice and should never be used without first consulting with a financial professional to determine what may be best for your individual needs.

The publisher and the author do not make any guarantee or other promise as to any results that may be obtained from using the content of this book. You should never make any investment decision without first consulting with your own financial advisor and conducting your own research and due diligence. To the maximum extent permitted by law, the publisher and the author disclaim any and all liability in the event any information, commentary, analysis, opinions, advice and/or recommendations contained in this book prove to be inaccurate, incomplete or unreliable, or result in any investment or other losses.

Content contained or made available through this book is not intended to and does not constitute legal advice or investment advice and no attorney-client relationship is formed. The publisher and the author are providing this book and its contents on an "as is" basis. Your use of the information in this book is at your own risk.

TABLE OF CONTENTS

TABLE OF CONTENTS 4

INTRODUCTION 6

CHAPTER 1 9
   Identifying Your Financial Freedom Goals. 9

CHAPTER 2 17
   Optimal Wealth Formula to Live the Lifestyle of Your Dreams. 17

CHAPTER 3 22
   How to Grow Your Money Through Investing. 22

CHAPTER 4 27
   Explore The Foreclosure Industry. 27

CHAPTER 5 32
   Leveraging the Cash of Your Creditors. 32

CHAPTER 6 35
   Establish A Home-Based Business To Retire Early. 35

CHAPTER 7 42
   Opt for Freedom Over Debt. 42

CHAPTER 8 47
   Ten-Point Plan to Regain Financial Control and Protect Your Family's Future. 47

CHAPTER 9 55

Make Your Future A Place Of Fun And Fortune. 55

CHAPTER 10 59

It's Time for You to Rule! 59

CONCLUSION. 62

INTRODUCTION.

Building wealth is not something that many young people in their forties consider when they begin receiving paychecks. However, starting to accumulate wealth early in life is one of the best steps you can take to ensure a prosperous financial future.

The primary reason is compound interest. The more time your money earns interest, the more money you will earn. As your balance increases, the interest you earn increases proportionately. While it may not appear that you are making much additional money, the difference can be significant when considering the entire amount of interest earned over thirty or forty years.

Beginning early also provides a benefit in that the earlier you start, the more risk you can afford to take. Individuals who start saving 10 years before retirement, for example, must invest in assets that will provide them with enough funds to live on in a short period.

You can take on more significant risks when you are young since you have more time to ride out market downturns or recover from poor investing decisions. However, it is often the riskier investments that yield the highest gains.

When you develop a plan for wealth accumulation as a young person, you can avoid making some of the most common blunders. To begin, you should establish an emergency fund. Whenever possible, avoid incurring debt.

Create and adhere to a budget. Regularly save a portion of each paycheck and invest. If you take these easy steps, which most people do not consider until they reach middle age, you will be ahead of the game.

Young folks who intend to begin their wealth accumulation plan should acquire as much knowledge as possible. The more knowledge you learn, the better off you will be. Investing and developing a financial plan can be perplexing, and you want to ensure that you are making the best decisions possible.

When developing your wealth development strategy, it may be beneficial to attend a wealth-building seminar. Wealth-building seminars are offered by industry specialists who can guide you in the proper direction.

If you are a young person in his/her forties who has begun to plan for your financial future, you have already made the first step toward financial success. Wealth creation is entirely dependent on information and strategy. With just a little forethought, you can be well on your way to financial freedom.

CHAPTER 1

Identifying Your Financial Freedom Goals.

When you ask individuals what they want most in life, they will almost always say they want to be rich, wealthy, or financially independent. Some of them will tell you they wish to live in a large house or mansion with a large backyard swimming pool, gold-plated faucets, a butler and/or a maid, and so on, but these are mainly merely fantasies of what riches is.

Indeed, many affluent individuals and millionaires drive reliable and luxurious but not necessarily flashy automobiles, live in well-designed but not too large homes, and do not constantly purchase the most costly clothing from the hottest designers du jour.

Indeed, if you ask these individuals why they want wealth in the first place, nearly all of them will state that they desire wealth to have more freedom in life.

What is your financial freedom goal?

Do you aspire to live the extravagant lifestyle represented on Entertainment Tonight, Access Hollywood, E! or VH1?

Do you wish to amass a considerable sum of money to explore the world?

Do you want enough money to maintain your current standard of living if you were to lose your work unexpectedly?

All these aspirations are achievable, although some will require more wealth accumulation than others.

Financial freedom is the capacity to accumulate sufficient wealth to enable you to leave your job and never be required to work again to maintain your lifestyle. Now, this will vary according to individual circumstances.

Suppose your lifestyle entails owning a large house with two luxury automobiles, taking many holidays each year, and purchasing an abundance of expensive clothing, jewelry and gadgets. In that case, your income is either extremely high, or you have leveraged yourself to the hilt in debt.

Moreover, if your lifestyle is more modest, you live in a condo or small house and keep your expenses low, you can survive on a mid-five-figure income. However, how can you determine what you require to achieve financial freedom?

According to R. Buckminster Fuller, wealth is calculated by the quantity of money saved divided by the period required to maintain your current lifestyle if you were suddenly laid off or lost your work.

For instance, if you saved $10,000 and could survive on it for five months, you would be considered wealthy for five months. If you saved $40,000 and could live on $2,000 a month, you would be wealthy for 20 months.

On the other hand, what if you could use those funds to create an income stream that would make you indefinitely wealthy?

This can be accomplished through passive income. Passive income is money that you receive without having to work for it. In other words, you earn money while sleeping. Passive income is typically generated through your own business, real estate, or investments in stocks or bonds.

Establishing a new business.

Many individuals have amassed money through the establishment of their businesses. Typically, they began by engaging in a passion they enjoyed, such as baking or arts and crafts, and charging for their products or services. You can do the same thing. The simplest method to get started is to sell your old unwanted items on eBay.

Many individuals began their home-based enterprises by selling their old junk on eBay to discover profitability. They would then collect used stuff from yard sales, Salvation Army thrift stores, and Goodwill and resale them profitably. If you are an internet-aware individual, you can earn money by selling other people's products via affiliate networks.

Affiliate programs enable you to sell things from other people's websites in exchange for a commission on each sale made via your website or blog. Clickbank, Linkshare, and Commission Junction are all good locations to start exploring for affiliate programs.

Earn money in real estate.

Real estate is one of the most prevalent ways for the typical person to accumulate money. While real estate has been an extremely popular way to earn any money in recent years, it appears as though we are on the cusp of a housing bubble poised to burst.

Most of this housing bubble can be traced to the process of flipping homes, in which individual purchases a home or condo with a large mortgage to resell it later on at a profit due to price appreciation. A large portion of this was promoted via late-night television infomercials.

While these tactics are effective and can earn you a significant amount of money in a short period, they do have certain disadvantages. First, it is not always a reliable source of passive income, and second, you may find yourself without buyers if the market peaks prematurely.

Of course, the time-honored method of profiting from real estate is to acquire rental homes. You purchase a building with two or three flats or a small apartment complex and rent out the remaining space to renters.

If you structure your mortgage and rents properly, your renters' rent payments will cover the cost of the monthly mortgage, taxes, and insurance, leaving you with additional money to spend.

It is not uncommon in some locations to earn a significant rental income from a reasonably priced apartment building. Some people make their livelihood solely by providing homes for others.

Investing in equities and bonds to generate passive income.

While this is a more straightforward option to get passive income than real estate, it requires more capital and requires you to understand stocks and bonds well enough to remain with your investment.

Dividends provide a passive income in this scenario. In other words, whether you purchase stock, treasury bills, or bonds, the corporation that issued the stock (or the United States Treasury Department in the case of bonds) will pay you a cash dividend.

This is in the form of a few cents per share or a nominal interest rate, but if you purchase a sufficient number of shares or bonds, this can provide a substantial income.

In some situations, it will give you a high-interest rate or yield, as it is often referred to as, which is often far more than bank savings. For instance, you invest $400,000 in equities that yield a 12-percent yearly dividend. Also, you retain ownership of the underlying stock, which you can sell for profit or hold until maturity in the case of bonds.

This stock would pay you $48,000 in dividends. Assume you hold this stock for five years, and it appreciates to $650,000, at which point you decide to sell. Not only would you have received $48,000 for each of the previous five years, but you would also have earned a capital gain of $250,000. (before commissions and taxes).

Of course, this is a brief overview of how to achieve financial freedom. If you live frugally, you may likely achieve financial freedom more rapidly by investing in income-producing real estate or starting your own business. If you desire a more lavish lifestyle, you may need to develop a comprehensive wealth-building strategy.

CHAPTER 2

Optimal Wealth Formula to Live the Lifestyle of Your Dreams.

There are many methods to generate this dynamic residual income, including owning rental property, receiving royalties on an invention or creative work, or working from home with a business that relies on residual income to cover its bills.

For instance, creative work generates residual revenue. Every year, authors such as JK Rowling and Tom Clancy and musicians such as Paul McCartney and Bob Dylan earn money on work they completed years ago. After their death, the income will continue to accrue to their estate. It's fantastic, and you, too, may earn in the same way with the correct home business selection.

Money in a bank would do the same function. Assume you desired a monthly income of $5000 to be able to do whatever you pleased. At a net interest rate of 5%, you would want at least $1.2 million in the bank. With taxes and other deductions, you would have needed to make roughly $2 million. How long will you work to earn that $1.2 million?

Thousands of people just like you are quietly amassing riches while working from home, even while sleeping. Are you going to join them?

This isn't a get-rich-quick scheme but a guaranteed and consistent income opportunity that thousands of people just like you have demonstrated works. It takes effort and determination, especially at first and sometimes for the full force to kick in.

I feel that life is too short to pause and make choices to progress in any endeavor.

Which one will you select?

Maintain the typical 45-year work schedule or create your own new residual income stream and watch it grow! In contrast to linear income, your net income has no ceiling. Did you know that 20% of millionaires obtained their wealth in this method?

Unsurprisingly, Anthony Robbins, Robert G Allen, Donald Trump, and Robert Kiyosaki are fervent proponents of constructing this ideal wealth formula with residual income streams.

Too many small business owners will declare, "I haven't taken a vacation in four years." Their businesses run them, not vice versa, as it should be. Whether you have been in business for a while or just starting, the sooner you start thinking about and implementing a strategy for increasing passive income, the sooner you'll attain personal and financial freedom.

You build freedom, not just a business, with your work-from-home, assuming you choose the correct one. You can generate a consistent revenue stream for months, years, or perhaps your entire life by working just once as you get compensated repeatedly for a one-time effort.

Wouldn't it be lovely to get paid hundreds of times for each hour worked?

To have this ideal riches formula operate in your favor while you build your passport to wealth.

What impact can it have on your life?

What kind of lifestyle would you lead?

It is time to begin the process of transformation. You could continue doing what you've always done and end up with the same result, but is that what you want? Inquire.

What am I doing now?

Where would I like to be?

What is the most efficient route for me to take?

Which would YOU prefer to do if you had the choice?

Receive payment once for work performed or received payment often - maybe for years or even the rest of your life - for work performed just once, via residual income? The choice is yours to make.

CHAPTER 3

How to Grow Your Money Through Investing.

While investing is one of the most effective strategies to achieve financial freedom, success requires specific skills and knowledge. Along with your knowledge and abilities, you must be willing to "take risks."

Do not be scared to take risks since you can control and limit them by arming yourself with the necessary skills and knowledge. As the adage goes, investing requires knowledge to avoid capital loss.

Before Investing.

Before investing, ensure that you have prepared the following essential items. Ascertain that all of your debts and liabilities have been satisfied. Before investing, ensure that you have a cash reserve or emergency reserves in place to assist you in case of an emergency so that you never have to withdraw your investment.

The recommended quantity of emergency money is three to six months' worth of income. Thus, if your monthly income is $2,500, you should have $15,000 in emergency funds that will last you six months.

Also, you should be required to purchase life insurance. A life insurance policy is a safeguard. You need life insurance if something tragic occurs to you. In the event of your death, life insurance may assist your family in recouping financial damages.

The recommended amount of life insurance is at least three years' worth of your annual income. If your yearly income is $60,000, you should purchase life insurance with a face value of $18,000 that is effective for three years to assist your family in recovering from financial losses.

After you've settled your obligations, established an emergency fund, and purchased insurance, it's time to determine your risk tolerance.

Determine Your Tolerance for Risk.

It always depends on your age; if you're still young, you can take a high risk, while those in their mid-40s to 50s should take a moderate risk, and those in their 50s and beyond should only consider low-risk investments.

Money market funds, term deposits, and bonds are all suitable assets for investors seeking a low-risk environment.

Bonds and equities are acceptable assets for those seeking a medium-risk profile.

You can invest exclusively in stock stocks if you want to take a significant risk.

Set a financial goal.

After determining your risk tolerance, you must establish a financial goal. What is the purpose of investing? It is a goal in which you should understand the aim of your investments and the monthly or annual costs associated with them.

When should you begin investing, and how do you intend to liquidate your holdings?

Decide to Invest.

A strategy is beneficial only if it is implemented. You will never get a return on your investment if you do not follow through on your strategy. You must act; take one step at a time.

Everything is straightforward, even more so if you genuinely desire to build your money. You should not be frightened to do so from account opening through account financing and if you decide to invest in the stock market. Consult a financial counselor or financial expert; advisors are available in banks and investment firms.

Saving money is beneficial since it instills the habit of money management. You will also be a disciplined investor if you are a diligent saver. Each month, set aside money from your pay or income to finance an investment account, such as mutual funds or a stockbroker account.

CHAPTER 4

Explore The Foreclosure Industry.

What is a foreclosure?

To describe a foreclosure, we must look at what happens when a borrower doesn't follow the conditions of the loan contract or agreement. The borrower has failed to repay the loan, and now the lender has the legal authority to seize the property to recoup the lost revenue from the repossession sale.

Not all foreclosures are created equal. Foreclosures come in different forms, including mortgage foreclosures, trust deed foreclosures, and strict foreclosures.

When a borrower obtains a loan from a bank, and a promissory note is issued, this is referred to as a mortgage foreclosure. This note details the loan's terms and conditions and specifies the monthly payment amount. Also, the promissory note specifies the monthly payment due date.

The loan is then secured by a mortgage contract, which serves as collateral for the debt. Often known as the mortgagee, the lender is granted specific rights if the borrower defaults on the loan. Until the debt is paid off, a lien is put on the house or property.

A trust deed foreclosure is another sort of foreclosure. This sort of contract involves the placement of the property's deed "in trust" with a third party, typically a title or trust corporation. Then some foreclosures are strictly enforced.

The lender legally and legitimately owns the home or property during this sort of foreclosure. The lender has the power to require the borrower to depart the property immediately upon the expiration of the borrower's right of redemption.

Many factors can contribute to a home falling victim to the foreclosure process. Interest rate increases, unemployment, and an unsteady economy could all be problems.

Also, the causes for foreclosure may be more personal, such as job relocation, death or incapacity, health, and medical difficulties, divorce, or a failed business enterprise. Many factors can contribute to a distressed homeowner.

There are various ways to acquire a home or property that is in some stage of foreclosure. Investors can purchase directly from the homeowner, which reduces the need for investors to compete with one another. Alternatively, buying via a public auction is a possibility.

When purchasing at auction, the homeowner is not involved in any negotiations. Another option is to purchase the real estate-owned property (REO) following the auction. In this case, you would interact directly with the bank or other lender and their agents.

When payment is not made on the agreed-upon monthly due date, the foreclosure process formally begins. Typically, the date corresponds to the start of the mortgage payment billing cycle.

Payments that have been missed can typically be arranged with the bank or lender to be made later. This results in the accrual of late charges following the grace period. Between days 45 and 60, the lender sends a certified letter or letter of intent to the borrower seeking payment.

Also, the letter specifies that the borrower is in breach of contract and that the home or property is at risk of foreclosure. After ninety days, the case is submitted to the foreclosure department, which files the required legal documentation.

As investors, capitalizing on these homes and properties might result in significant wealth and financial freedom. The plan is composed of three components. The first step is to locate bargains.

Following that, it's a matter of going forward and making an offer that is accepted—finally, cashing it in, whether that means wholesaling and handing over the property to the investor in exchange for a check, renting it out, or selling it in the future.

CHAPTER 5

Leveraging the Cash of Your Creditors.

Most adults in their forties make poor financial decisions. It takes a tremendous deal of discipline to invest that extra money in something that will provide you with larger returns in the short, medium, and long term.

The credit card sector is the most profitable in the United States. The average person is incapable of making sound financial decisions. Creditors' primary target group (prey) is 18-year-olds who lack financial literacy and have little to no credit history.

Each year, millions of Americans apply for new credit cards regardless of their gender, race, ethnic origin, or disability. All that is required is that you are a United States citizen and at least 18 years of age.

What gets me every time is when creditors enlist those extremely young and naive individuals in a contract/agreement, and they foolishly squander every cent remaining on the card's credit line on dumb things that will do them no good.

Creditors will pretend to be your closest friend to squeeze every penny from your wallet with high adjustable interest rates and all the contingencies listed in small print above the applicant's signature.

I concentrate on today's younger generation solely because it is entirely natural for a young person to lack the financial intelligence necessary to succeed in life and avoid financial peril. The elderly should have learned this lesson early through their experiences and economic hardships, but most do not regrettably.

A young person's primary advantage is leveraging the creditors' money to earn more money and pay off the credit card each month. You would need to acquire the necessary expertise and develop a good plan to accomplish this.

Knowledge - Knowledge is powerful but only when it is applied effectively. However, before you acquire knowledge, you must develop an investment attitude by reading inspirational investor books.

Once you've developed the proper mindset, you'll be so enthused and driven that you'll be willing to study. When taught correctly, it will reduce risk and give you more significant and more sensible financial decisions and opportunities.

My best suggestion is to seek out those who excel in the field you wish to work in and pick their brains. There is a trick to picking the brains of financially successful people, and you must learn how to use it to your advantage.

Sources of information - The resources you need to understand how to achieve financial freedom are all around you. Your closest buddy is Google; look for the greatest investment books, purchase them at your local book store, and keep up with current events by reading the Wall Street Journal. Attend a lecture to educate yourself and to network.

CHAPTER 6

Establish A Home-Based Business To Retire Early.

Cash flow is the most important term in the revenue industry. Leverage is the second important term. Leverage is the reason why some people get wealthy while others do not. Less than 5% of all Americans are wealthy because only 5% understand how to leverage their wealth.

Among the well-known kinds of leverage is borrowing money. Millions of people are in financial peril as a result of debt leverage being used against them. Excellent debt makes you affluent, whereas bad debt keeps you impoverished.

Your intellect, the most powerful form of leverage in the world, can make you wealthy or impoverished.

Beliefs.

Individuals who are wealthy use wealthy language, whereas those who are impoverished use impoverished language. Your mind may be your most valuable asset or your greatest liability.

The distinction between wealthy and impoverished people is that poor people say "I can't afford it" more often than wealthy people. If you want to retire young and wealthy, you must use your thinking to your advantage, not against you. Forbes magazine defines wealth as having annual revenue of $1 million or more.

The problem with working on a job is that it obstructs your path to prosperity. Most people intend to be impoverished. That is why so many people claim, "When I retire, my income will decrease."

In other words, they're saying, "I intend to work hard my entire life and retire impoverished." Today, millions of workers rely on their pension plans, including 401(k) and IRA accounts.

Employees are now in charge of their retirement. During the Industrial Revolution, it was up to the firm or the government to look after your financial requirements once your workdays ended. These Information Age pension schemes have one fatal weakness.

The fault is that most of these plans are indexed to the stock market, and as you may have noticed, stock markets rise and fall. Promising to work diligently for the rest of your life is a lousy strategy.

For many baby boomers, time, our most valuable resource, is running out. In reality, less than 5% of the US population is wealthy because 95% wishes to be wealthy, but only 5% takes action.

The three primary assets that make persons affluent and enable them to retire early are as follows:

1. Real estate

2. Intangible assets

3. Enterprises

We all have concerns. The distinction is in how we respond to those inquiries. If you can adapt your words and thoughts to those of the wealthy, retiring young and wealthy will be straightforward. The greatest obstacle you face is overcoming your self-doubt and lethargy.

Your self-distrust and sloth define who you are. If you intend to alter who you are, you must confront your self-doubt and sloth. Your self-doubt and laziness are the factors that keep you small. It is your self-doubt and sloth that prevent you from living the life you desire.

Nobody is standing in your way except you and your self-doubts. It's simple to maintain the status quo. It's easy to remain unchanged. Most people opt to remain the same throughout their life. By confronting your self-doubt and laziness, you will uncover the key to your liberation.

Many people do not do what they are capable of doing because they lack a compelling "why." Once you've determined your "why," it's easy to decide on your own "how-to" to riches; rather than delving within to identify their own "why" for wanting to become wealthy, most people seek the simplest path to prosperity and the problem with the simplest path is that it often leads to a dead end.

Three further paths to immense wealth are as follows:

1. Improving business abilities

2. Improving money management abilities

3. Improving investment abilities

If you find yourself debating a fantastic concept, you may wish to refrain from debating. When someone says, 'I can't afford it' or 'I can't do it,' to something they desire, they have a significant problem.

Why on earth would someone say, "I can't do it" in response to something they desire? I was arguing about shielding myself from the heartache that dreaming huge aspirations may bring if not realized. I'd dreamed and blown up.

I realized I was arguing against another failure rather than against the aim. A hint: Years ago, I discovered that passion is a blend of love and hatred. Without a passion for something, it isn't easy to do anything. If you want something, pursue it with zeal.

Your life is energized by passion. If you wish for something you don't have, consider why you desire it and why you despise not having it. When you combine these two ideas, you'll find the motivation to rise from your seat and grab anything you require. I've heard many people remark, "Money does not buy happiness."

"How many of you wish to retire in your forties and be financially independent for the rest of your years? That sentence contains some truth. However, income allows me to spend more time doing things I enjoy and compensates others for what I despise. How many of you are considering early retirement?"

CHAPTER 7

Opt for Freedom Over Debt.

Too many people are in debt, which is hardly surprising because any quantity greater than zero is excessive. This is predominantly a development from the last quarter of the twentieth century, one of the Baby Boomer phenomena.

Prior generations were typically required to pay for what they purchased at the time of purchase, have a considerable amount of collateral, or have a third-party co-signer to purchase on time.

A farmer or rancher in the agricultural nineteenth century might purchase on time from the general store. They would repay their loans at the end of the season when their products or animals were harvested.

Initially, these general store merchants extended credit to the consumer. Then, in the early twentieth century, credit cards were invented and became very ubiquitous by the mid-century. [creditcards.com]

Credit cards were accepted for payment since they could only be provided to people with a good credit history. They were distributed more freely than Halloween treats in the late twentieth and early twenty-first centuries. They were even delivered unannounced door to door.

The cause for this explosion in credit card use during this period was that not enough individuals were spending enough money to satisfy businesses that manufactured items and supplied services. The consumer desired to spend all or nearly all their money. This was too restrictive. It was intolerable and could not continue.

Any business that wants to expand and thrive needs customers to spend more than they can afford. We dwell in a world ruled by plastic credit cards. We have returned to the past, owing to our souls to the company store (read consumer debt) Tennessee Ernie Ford sang about in his classic Sixteen Tons.

To reduce debt, it is important to understand how it accumulates, when want exceeds the need, when more is believed to be better when more is not enough, when impatience will not wait when buying is not preceded by browsing when the cost is not taken into the price and so on.

There is a widespread misperception that having what one desires and having it when one desires will bring happiness. Understanding this myth will put an end to its belief and enable behavior to alter. It will just add stress and anxiety to the process of determining how to pay for items bought.

The answer is money, but not in the conventional sense. When it comes to money, there exist two considerations. Having adequate money is the key to debt elimination, need fulfillment, and financial security to enjoy happiness.

Spending money on fundamental necessities such as food, clothing, and shelter is a wise investment. Everything else that can be purchased will become outmoded; will deteriorate over time to the point of deterioration, or become unneeded and so discarded. The money used to buy these items will also be deleted.

What is the goal of all this spending, most of which are made with money we anticipate having in the future, as evidenced by the usage of credit cards? Money's ultimate worth is not in what it can purchase but in what it can deliver. It just provides temporary pleasure.

Money can be accumulated by saving it, but its value will diminish over time due to inflation; consequently, it must be invested and left alone to appreciate and compound. This will ensure financial security, mental tranquility, and genuine happiness. It will bring about Liberty.

I'm reminded of a long-forgotten Robert Frost poem titled The Road Not Taken. It begins, Two paths split in a yellow wood, and I took the less traveled one, which made all the difference. It fits in the sense that liberty is defined as the ability to choose one's way of life.

Two pathways diverge as well when journeying through one's financial life. One road is lined with all of life's joys, with self-indulgences galore just waiting for the traveler to enjoy. Credit paves the way to serfdom, where Freedom is constrained solely by self-imposed financial responsibilities.

A second path involves self-control and self-imposed constraints on pleasure but is lined with abundant wealth, success, and good fortune and leads to affluence where financial security and freedom prevail.

Each and everyone selects his or her path. Live without making excuses or regretting your choice. Prosperity is only a short distance down the road. All that is required is to take the correct route.

CHAPTER 8

Ten-Point Plan to Regain Financial Control and Protect Your Family's Future.

This chapter summarizes a ten-point tested and proven plan you can adopt to regain complete financial control and protect your family's future. Read on.

a) Eliminate debt

Before doing anything else, credit card debt, overdrafts, and loans, particularly secured loans, must be paid off. You can never accumulate riches for yourself or your family while paying monthly interest on debts.

Transfer your bills to less expensive alternatives, particularly 0% credit cards, if you can obtain them and make sacrifices today to pay off your obligations as quickly as feasible. The sooner you pay them off, the sooner you may begin saving and earning money.

b) Ascertain that you have a safety net of savings and some liquid funds for investing.

If you do not have sufficient 'liquid' cash saved up to cover immediate costs, there is no use in investing for the future. By 'liquid,' I mean 'easy to obtain.'

This implies you should have enough money in a savings account to sustain you and your family for a few months if everything goes wrong. Calculate how much money you need to spend each month to have a roof over your head and food in your mouths, multiply it by three, and set aside that money in an account that you do not access unless an emergency occurs.

c) Complete your mortgage payment

Paying off your mortgage early is among the safest and most tax-efficient investments you can make. It provides you with the tremendous freedom of being mortgage-free; it is a tax-free investment because any money you overpay on your mortgage saves you the total amount of interest, in contrast to savings accounts, which tax the interest you pay.

It is among the safest investments you can make because you pay it off entirely when paying off your mortgage.

Consider the following figures: Monthly payments on a £100,000 repayment mortgage at 5% interest would be £584.59 over 25 years, with a total interest payment of £75,377.

However, if you shorten the payment term to 15 years, your monthly payments would be £790.79, but you would pay just £42,342.20 in interest during that period, a savings of £33,034.80. (Savills)

d) Distribute your wagers

To be safe, diversify your investments across asset classes (shares, property, cash, bonds, and so on).

Nothing is certain in investing. Don't put your eggs in one basket. Nobody possesses a crystal ball, and no one can predict what will occur in the future. Nothing, not even houses, is as secure as houses. You cannot rely on any single asset class to accumulate a sizable sum of money to draw a comfortable income in the future.

e) Maintain consistency

As with biological functions, it's a good idea to remain consistent when saving and investing! If you only have a small amount of money left over each month, it's far better in the long term to set up a monthly standing order from your bank account to investment, so the money is invested before you see it.

Also, by investing at regular intervals, you benefit from what is known as 'pound cost averaging,' which means that you capture the ups and downs of a volatile investment (such as the stock market), which smooths out to an average, respectable return over time.

f) Acquaint yourself with the facts and think for yourself - do not follow the herd.

Money management is similar to eating a balanced diet. You do not need to be a nutritionist to know how to eat healthfully. Still, you need to understand some fundamental facts about fruits and vegetables, vitamins, protein, and minerals to plan a balanced and healthy diet.

It's the same with money management. You don't need to be a licensed financial adviser, but you should understand how money works.

Therefore, spend a few minutes each week reading the Daily Express's money section. Acquire some knowledge about saving and investing by visiting the mine, Money Magpie, or The Motley Fool.

We would be significantly wealthier if we spent as much time investigating financial matters as we do researching the next flat-screen TV to buy or which new smartphone to purchase.

g) Invest in inexpensive, straightforward products that you understand.

It is feasible to earn a reasonable profit in the stock market if you invest long-term and stick to simple items with modest fees. Index-tracking funds (often referred to as 'Trackers') and exchange-traded funds are the two primary products that come within this category (ETFs).

These investments are typically managed by computer programs rather than human fund managers needing a new Porsche Boxster for Christmas. They monitor stock market indices, commodities (oil or sugar), or even entire countries (like China, Brazil, or Russia).

h) Reduce the tax

Each year, ensure that you take advantage of all available tax-avoidance strategies. After all, why would you spend all that time and effort earning a living and considering prudent investments just to lose a large portion of it due to tax evasion?

Pensions and products from the National Savings and Investments Company and certain specialized investment funds are tax-free and well worth considering. That so, it's important to consider the whole net profit first, rather than pursuing something because it's tax-free. Occasionally, even with the tax incentive, the returns are still insufficient to justify the investment.

i) Safeguard your family's finances

If you have a family or dependents, ensure that you have enough life insurance to keep them afloat if you cannot provide for them. This is one place where you cannot cut corners. Ascertain that the mortgage would be paid and that they would be sustained in the event of your absence.

j) Change your investments as your circumstances change.

Your investment requirements alter as you age. Whether you are in your forties, you can afford to invest in riskier items that should provide you with positive returns over time. As you age, though, it's prudent to invest some of your money in more stable entities that are less profitable but also safer.

Also, approximately five years before you plan to retire, it is a good idea to 'lifestyle' your investments and begins shifting your money away from more volatile, 'growth' products (shares, property, commodities, etc.) and toward more stable investments such as savings accounts, bonds, and gilts to capture the huge gains you have made over the years and maintain them even if markets fall.

CHAPTER 9

Make Your Future A Place Of Fun And Fortune.

If you want to achieve financial freedom in your forties while also building generational wealth, you should choose a sector in high demand now and for decades to come. The travel industry satisfies these criteria. Each year, the United States spends $1.3 million on travel. This equates to around $2.5 million each minute.

Travel, as you may have guessed! Worldwide, about $7 million in travel is purchased, most of it online and that figure is increasing. It will quadruple in the next few years as the baby boomer generation prepares to retire. What do they wish to pursue further after working, retiring, saving and raising their families?

When you examine the travel sector now, you will notice that many multibillion-dollar enterprises (mainly online) did not exist even ten years ago. Every day, new businesses vie for a piece of that sizable and valuable pie. The following are three tendencies that contribute to travel being one of the finest ways for the regular individual to enter the game of turning enjoyment into money.

The Internet's first trend is e-commerce. Consumers have grown increasingly comfortable and adept with obtaining many of their requirements online over the last decade.

Even if you shop offline, the Internet is an excellent resource for researching anything you wish to purchase. The same research capabilities are now becoming a popular activity for travelers.

Travel agents used to be a good source of recommendations for places to stay and hang out when planning a trip. Many people now book their leisure trips online. You may read about other people's travel experiences on dozens of websites nowadays. Travel purchases made online are already costing consumers billions of dollars.

The baby boomer generation is causing the second major demographic shift. The baby-boomer generation has been a significant influence since the 1950s.

They influenced a variety of industries, including automotive, home renovation, and, most recently, travel. There are 79 million baby boomers in the United States and nearly 1 billion around the world. For the next two decades, they will be retiring one every eight seconds.

Home-based enterprises are the third trend. Millions of Americans today have a home-based business to augment or possibly replace their primary job. With its large and mid-sized enterprises downsizing and outsourcing to other countries, corporate America may not be the best path to financial security, let alone financial freedom. Entrepreneurs have a Plan B for their financial futures with home-based business prospects.

There is an incredible opportunity in the travel industry to manage a full-fledged internet travel agency from the convenience of your home office. The tax reductions alone are a significant benefit when it comes to increasing your net worth.

Economists and entrepreneurs agree that you want to be on the cutting edge of long-term trends, not fads. Travel on the Internet, facilitated by technologies accessible to small company owners, appears to be a fantastic possibility.

Conduct due diligence to identify a credible business that is capitalizing on this market shift. Then join the group of astute company entrepreneurs who travel, have fun, and earn money simultaneously.

CHAPTER 10

It's Time for You to Rule!

Our country continues to have individuals living in demeaning social situations; it continues to be destroyed by crime and preventable lifestyle ailments. Most people are still living paycheck to paycheck and pleading with the government for work.

While some have achieved upward mobility, they have not yet reached their full potential due to their effort to avoid drowning in a sea of debt. They are screaming for help to save them from themselves!

Regrettably, the solution to your situation does not lie with the government or others; it lies with you! Once you begin to rule yourself, your social and economic circumstances will begin to alter. Once that occurs, you will begin to attain and enjoy the economic prosperity our predecessors envisioned and fought for.

However, this is only possible if you begin today by reclaiming control of your two most valuable resources: time and money. That's correct; how you manage your time and money determines where you are today. Therefore, why don't you begin by ensuring that you're getting the most out of both?

Second, you must understand that "wealth" is created by accumulating income-producing assets - put, putting your money to work for you. Thus, accumulating wealth will be incredibly difficult if you do not set aside a portion of your salary to invest.

However, if you consistently set away a portion of your income for investing, you will discover that wealth generation is relatively simple.

It's quite straightforward. If you lack savings, you cannot invest, resulting in a lack of wealth growth, as you cannot invest what you lack. Thus, the first step is to begin saving money! Not often but regularly and methodically. This year, you should make it a point to save a percentage of each paycheck you receive.

If you earn $100.00 every week and spend the entire $100.00 each week, you will have nothing to show for your efforts. Nothing! Indeed, what were you doing, and for whom were you doing it? As you've given all your money out and compensated everyone but yourself!

You must continue to regard money as if it were milk; otherwise, you cannot accumulate wealth. Thus, how can you begin amassing wealth?

Start managing your costs in such a way that you can save a portion of everything you earn. Whatever happens, you should maintain your commitment to yourself, the determination to save your money until you invest it.

It's a matter of respecting yourself and believing in your future worth investing in. Purchase a copy of the "Taking Control of Your Money" workbook; it's an excellent resource for getting started.

CONCLUSION.

One of the most significant obstacles that most novices to the financial world face is their fear of investing. For decades, the stock market and investment portfolios have been the exclusive domain of a small percentage of the population: the wealthy, the highly entrepreneurial, or those with an economics degree. It has long been a field where knowledge is equated with power, and power equals a good, fat bank account.

Unfortunately, this kind of thinking offers few options for those with small savings accounts, limited knowledge of finance, or unwillingness to trust the existing system with their hard-earned money. Unfortunately, many people avoid seeking a financial advisor's advice for different personal and financial reasons, none of which is a barrier to a secure future.

One of the most significant impediments to investing is the widespread belief that you must have money to make money. To begin investing, you must have thousands of dollars set aside. After all, how can you consider investing if you're cannot save enough money to get started?

Although many types of accounts need a minimum commitment, you can also begin with a modest amount. While you may initially earn a lesser rate of return, small investments in bonds, common stocks, and IRAs are often simple to make, do not require large sums of money, and allow you to learn as you go, increasing your comfort level with investing you save more money.

I cannot access my funds in the event of an emergency. Another typical financial concern is that your money will be invested so that you will be unable to access it in the event of a medical or family emergency. While certain accounts (such as certificates of deposit) carry a high penalty for early withdrawal, others do not (like money market accounts).

The trick is to figure out which investments are the best fit for you and your lifestyle - there is no right or wrong method to do it. Often, it's ideal for working with a financial advisor who can assist you in developing a portfolio that is a solid mix of long-term savings and shorter-term investments that allow you greater control over your money.

I'm afraid I'm going to lose everything. When investing in the stock market, there is always a risk of losing or significantly reducing your savings. This is not a common occurrence, and it typically occurs to those who engage exclusively in high-risk investments.

When you invest prudently and with the supervision of a financial advisor who will diversify your assets across many various types of accounts, you have a very high chance of profiting over the following 10, twenty, thirty, or even forty years.

The trick is to approach investing as a long-term strategy; while you may not become independently wealthy next year, you will have something to fall back on when it comes time to retire.

The benefits of investing are too great to ignore, even if you lack a sizable savings account, are already in debt, or are unfamiliar with finances.

Your best course of action is to consult with a financial advisor who can advise you on what to do first and how to begin regaining control of your future. The greatest financial advisors will look beyond the balance in your bank account and will work with you each step of the way to ensure your comfort.

Thanks for Reading

Series: Financial Freedom at Any Age

1. Achieving Financial Freedom in your 20's
2. Achieving Financial Freedom in your 30's
3. Achieving Financial Freedom in your 40's
4. Achieving Financial Freedom in your 50's
5. Achieving Financial Freedom in your 60's
6. Achieving Financial Freedom in your 70's and beyond.
7. Achieving Financial Freedom in children
8. Achieving Financial Freedom in teenagers
9. Achieving Financial Freedom in college students.

www.ingramcontent.com/pod-product-compliance
Lightning Source LLC
Chambersburg PA
CBHW070313220526
45465CB00004B/1858